POWER
THOUGHTS
MOTIVATIONAL
FUEL
for SUCCESS

Bert Rodriguez

BALBOA.
PRESS
A DIVISION OF HAY HOUSE

Balboa Press books may be ordered through booksellers or by contacting:

Balboa Press
A Division of Hay House
1663 Liberty Drive
Bloomington, IN 47403
www.balboapress.com
1 (877) 407-4847

Because of the dynamic nature of the Internet, any web addresses or
links contained in this book may have changed since publication and
may no longer be valid. The views expressed in this work are solely those
of the author and do not necessarily reflect the views of the publisher,
and the publisher hereby disclaims any responsibility for them.

The author of this book does not dispense medical advice or prescribe the use
of any technique as a form of treatment for physical, emotional, or medical
problems without the advice of a physician, either directly or indirectly. The
intent of the author is only to offer information of a general nature to help
you in your quest for emotional and spiritual well-being. In the event you use
any of the information in this book for yourself, which is your constitutional
right, the author and the publisher assume no responsibility for your actions.

Any people depicted in stock imagery provided by Thinkstock are
models, and such images are being used for illustrative purposes only.
Certain stock imagery © Thinkstock.

Print information available on the last page.

ISBN: 978-1-5043-3921-6 (sc)
ISBN: 978-1-5043-3924-7 (e)

Balboa Press rev. date: 9/29/2015

It is customary in Tibetan Buddhism to begin books with a short poem, a Koan. Tradition states that if you can understand the Koan, reading the book is not necessary because the poem contains all the wisdom in the book.

As we're trying to see who we are
Our wishes and dreams seem so far

We wonder if all we are doing
Will get us to where we are going

Our plans for our quest we have sown
But life has some roads of its own

Be assured that your goals will appear
But the visions you see must stay clear

With passion and heartfelt desire
A life full of joy you'll acquire

This book is dedicated to Kathy Rivers who gave
me the needed push, space, and opportunity to
discover who I am so that I could appreciate, learn
to love myself, and pursue my purpose in life. It
is a gift for which I will forever be grateful.

The best way I can repay this invaluable gift is to pass
these thoughts on to you to motivate, inspire, encourage,
and empower the champion in all of you. We all face
difficult moments in this long, adventurous journey, and
I hope that you too may acquire the courage, strength,
and power needed to overcome life's challenges!

CONTENTS

ABOUT THE AUTHOR

The strength and success of anything you do are limited only by how much you are willing to sacrifice yourself in order to succeed.
—Bert Rodriguez

Master Bert Rodriguez has dedicated over 50 years to the study and understanding of our bodies—both its physical and mental aspects and the ability to control and use these to experience this adventure we call life.

From early childhood he has been on a journey to comprehend how our thoughts, emotions, and attitudes strongly influence our physical being, and how, in turn, this influences our lives, who we become, our purpose, and the final product of what we create and are able to share with our children, others, and future generations.

A consummate life coach, Master Rodriguez has an extensive background as a counselor and motivational speaker in the fields of positive attitude, self-hypnosis, and personal motivation. He has mentored and helped students and clients face themselves and their fears for over 45 years, empowering them to achieve success in their individual fields.

The student does not become a master without years of hard work, dedication, and study. During his journey in martial arts, Master Rodriguez has earned black belts—and four master degrees—in eight distinct styles. As a result, he has extensive knowledge of their foundations, backgrounds, histories, and the philosophies of Zen and its application. It is on this foundation that he has developed his Power Thoughts and philosophy that he shares with you today.

Master Rodriguez is also a highly respected trainer of world champions in the fields of kickboxing and boxing. He has coached and mentored numerous professionals and amateurs, sharing his mastery of martial arts techniques as well as his own style of Blending. In addition, he has trained members of the United States Drug Enforcement Administration, Metro Dade Police Academy, Broward County Sheriff's Office, and numerous individuals in various departments in the U.S. military and armed forces.

Harnessing his personal philosophy of strength of character and commitment to overcoming difficulties, Master Rodriguez has become a successful entrepreneur. He established Power Punch Promotions in South Florida, which opened and owned US #1 Fitness Centers in West Palm Beach, North Miami, and Dania, Florida, and US #1 Business Systems and Investments. In 2013, he became a published author with the release of his first book, Face Fear, Create Courage, achieving another personal goal.

Master Rodriguez has appeared and been featured on radio and television shows and networks, including 20/20, Dateline, CNN, NBC, CNBC, BBC, PBS, the Learning Channel, the Discovery Channel, Canadian Broadcasting, Telemundo, Univision, and others worldwide.

Ever a student of the universe and teacher of the willing, Master Rodriguez has most recently embarked on a journey to encapsulate the wisdoms collected over a course of life adventures and lessons. In the book, Power Thoughts, which you now possess, he shares these short thoughts and quotes, which have been an effective philosophy he has applied to his life and has imparted to family, clients, and those he has counseled through the years.

With Power Thoughts, Master Rodriguez expresses a mindset he has personally used—and has provided as a guide for others—to stay in control. Through contemplation, we can learn to redirect ourselves to a contented state of mind and a positive future.

INTRODUCTION

The two most important and valuable assets that we will ever possess are our physical and mental health! Our ability to understand, strengthen, nourish, and improve our capabilities to use them is crucial to our survival and growth. At an early age, I became intrigued with the power of the mind as well as the effects of a good diet for proper physical growth and strength. In later years—after being involved in the fitness business as well as training athletes, competitors, and world champions—I realized the correlation between proper physical nutrition and mental nutrition. In both cases, a diet that consists of good, clean, healthful ingredients is critical to reaching a high level of performance.

Over the years, I have mentored and trained top competitors—in sports and in other fields of endeavors, including business, careers of all types as well as with those just trying to be able to deal with their individual struggles. Through these experiences, I realized the importance self-control and, first and foremost, of feeding the mind with positive, encouraging, inspiring, and empowering thoughts. This is the foundation necessary to support the physical, or tangible, part of our lives through to any winning situation.

In my first published book, Face Fear, Create Courage, I discussed in the individual chapters the importance of The Power of Thought, The Power of Words, as well as the laws of Oriental wisdom known as Yin and Yang. It relates how everything in nature and the universe is comprised of seemingly opposing forces that constantly work together and are actually interconnected to create the necessary flow of life. This includes the balance and harmony we need to overcome our challenges.

I give an example that I immediately share with everyone I train, counsel, or teach about how our minds can trump the physical. It is relatively easy for us to walk a two- or three-foot-wide board that is placed on the ground. We can lean over the edge, even stick out a leg or an arm with little or no effort (or fear). But yet the same board placed 50 feet in the air becomes an obstacle of overwhelming proportion. Thoughts have an incredible power over everything we experience in life.

Our thoughts determine the way we interpret and create the successes and failures in our lives. No matter the size, strength, or quality of your physical body—or any tangible material at your disposal—the mind's ability to create, control, and use its resources to the nth power will determine the final result.

For this reason, it is important to supply the mind (as you would the body) with clean, positive, nourishing substances—or "mind food"—in order to have an efficient tool to successfully achieve whatever the goal may be. How do we "feed" the mind? Physical nutrition is important, but what led to the birth of this book is the necessity and benefit of Power Thoughts as an integral part of the "mind food" diet.

All the Power Thoughts that I share with you in this book (and in my blog), I also read and re-read to help remind me and empower me in my walk in life. Although I wrote them, they do not come from me. Instead, they come through me from a Universal Intelligence that is in every living thing on this planet and part of all of us. The more you absorb them, the more they will strengthen you and become part of your winning attitude. Take time to read, re-read, ingest, and contemplate on each individual thought before you continue to the next.

These Power Thoughts address scenarios we all encounter in different ways, and they present the opportunity to gain a different perspective on how to blend and be in harmony with the challenges, obstacles, and struggles of life. You will find that these Power Thoughts are a reflection of things you already know but haven't taken the time to realize (or reflect on the fact that you know them).

In addition to Power Thoughts, I will also share with you The Ten Steps to Success. I created this list over 40 years ago and have used in lectures and teaching. The Ten Steps to Success are presented in order of importance from one to ten. You can't focus on the tenth step until you have addressed the first—or break the sequence—if you want to use it effectively. I will give three examples using it in sequence to illustrate the process. I hope you enjoy and can efficiently find a way to use it in whatever your goal may be.

In order to really appreciate and understand the layout of what will be presented in both the Power Thoughts and the Ten Steps to Success, I felt the book should begin with an overview of what has been taught in the East for thousands of years. Chapter One will guide you through the Dynamics of Yin and Yang. It is a philosophy of thought that has helped me truly understand every subject I have ventured to learn and, as you will see, it is at the base of everything in the universe. As I previously mentioned, it was an important chapter in my first publication Face Fear, Create Courage and I feel it will be beneficial to you as you absorb each of the Power Thoughts.

My hope is that Power Thoughts will provide the fuel needed to nourish and feed your mind.

Enjoy.

CHAPTER ONE

THE DYNAMICS OF YIN AND YANG

In every disaster there lies the seed of a potential benefit.

This section of the book contains the groundwork to help you develop a clearer and more proficient game plan for your life—one that can help you understand reality, the universal laws of physics, their relation to the human body and mind, and your interaction with the world around you.

To truly grasp these principles and the fundamental concepts that are the foundation of our universe, we need go no further than the laws and the teachings that have permeated Asian culture, known as the yin and yang.

This symbol, which is associated with Eastern culture, originated thousands of years ago and is a profound way of seeing the way nature exists. It is at the foundation of everything we see. It is at the root of mathematics, because without "nothingness," what is cannot be. (Binary arithmetic—based on one and zero—has made computers possible.)

The principles of yin and yang are more apparent in our lives than we can imagine. They represent the perpetual balance that exists in the universe and our lives. We need to understand their meaning and tap into the power they use effortlessly.

Nature exists in perfect balance, for everything it takes away it gives you something in return. Balance and harmony are the foundations of wisdom.

The Yin and Yang Symbol

Whenever I begin a class, I ask students, including some that have studied Asian cultures, philosophies, and the concept of yin and yang, if they are familiar with this symbol. They typically answer with: "It stands for hard and soft" or "it stands for male and female." Although these answers are correct, they are only a small part of its complexity.

It is a symbol that represents an idea that everything we know is governed by the underlying truth that all things are made up of seemingly opposite positive and negative energies that continuously blend together in harmony with one another. Everything in the universe is affected in some way by this principle of opposites blending harmoniously.

The art of life is not seen as holding to yang and banishing yin but as keeping the two in balance because there cannot be one without the other. This is right; this is wrong. I like this; I don't like that. According to Buddhist beliefs, these dualities are the source of suffering and problems. Dividing up our world in this way is false thinking. Things do not either exist or not exist; they do both. All computations were revolutionized by the recognition that "nothing" was "something." It is the law of perpetuity that makes our continued existence possible.

The Harmony of Opposites

Notice that day turns into night and night to day as does summer and winter, life and death, as well as all things in nature. Opposites blend by becoming each other or being a part of each other, thus the dot of black in the white and the dot of white in the black that we see in the yin and yang symbol illustrated.

In other words, when it's daytime, we seek the shade. When it's nighttime, we turn on the lights. When it's hot, we look for cool. When it's cold, we seek the warmth. When it rains, we wait for sunny days. When it's dry, we pray for rain. When we're young, we want to be older. And when we get old, we want to be younger, and so on and so on.

They are not just harmoniously blending constantly with each other but continuously exist within one another. We should accept and appreciate this and that all things need to be in harmony to continue the smooth cycle of life. To make it easier to understand this, here is a partial list of simple examples in different categories. See if you can add some more to this list.

The Harmony of Opposites (table)

Day	Night
Sun	Moon
Summer	Winter
Spring	Fall
Hot	Cold
Soft	Hard
Rough	Smooth
In	Out
Up	Down
Left	Right
Relaxed	Tense
Addition	Subtraction
Division	Multiplication
Action	Reaction
Straight	Circular
Short	Tall
Light	Dark
Inhale	Exhale
Rich	Poor
Loud	Quiet
Full	Empty
Happiness	Sadness
Love	Hate
Pain	Pleasure

Mind	Body
Debits	Credits
Laughing	Crying
Cowardice	Courage
Health	Sickness
Strength	Weakness

These things endlessly permeate our existence and thoughts. I share with my students that these are all individually things we know, and yet we never put them together.

Everything is different, but everything is the same in some way. The human body is also affected in its duality of mental and physical. We can all know what it takes to lose weight, to quit smoking, to stop an addiction. But knowing and doing are two different things. Knowing is only half the equation. The mind and body must become one in order to accomplish our goals.

Regardless of the subject, to be able to comprehend it better, we need to dissect it to the most common denominator—establish a sense of relation or comparison to it. This can be seen as a way to see the complexity of our universe in its simplest terms.

As you read this book, your mind absorbs it as chapters, pages, paragraphs, sentences, words, letters, dots, and commas, and yet at the same time, you reverse the process to ingest the information.

In mathematics, we look for common denominators to solve equations; in chemistry, we see matter as molecules,

molecules to atoms, atoms to protons and neutrons. Recently, DNA has further increased our understanding of ourselves. In war, if you can divide your enemy into separate groups, they will be easier to conquer.

The way to eat an elephant is one bite at a time.
—Old proverb

You can deal with problems and fears in the same way—one day at a time—by breaking them into parts and by taking on the small ones first. All the Power Thoughts in some way will refer to this phenomenon throughout this study. Keep this in mind and it will help you better understand the different subjects in each of the quotes. Note that although these ideas may sometimes be easier to grasp when they are applied to tangible (either visible or physical) strategies, they can also be effective strategies for dealing with verbal or mental conflict.

There are numerous examples throughout these chapters. Look for them. Study them and the ways you can apply them to yourself.

The Bible is about good and evil. The book of Ecclesiastes, which was authored by King Solomon, a man God blessed with the gift of great wisdom, states this:

There is a time for everything and a season for every activity under heaven:

> A time to be born, and a time to die; A
> time to plant, and time to uproot;
> A time to kill, and a time to heal;
> A time to tear down, and a time to build;
> A time to weep, and a time to laugh;
> A time to mourn, and a time to dance;
> A time to scatter stones, and a time to
> gather them;
> A time to embrace, and a time to refrain;

> A time to keep, and a time to throw away;
> A time to tear, and a time to mend;
> A time to speak, and a time to be silent;
> A time to love, and a time to hate;
> A time for war, and a time for peace.

After facing so many instances where I tried to make things happen the way I wanted, this passage helped me to learn one of the greatest lessons in my life and brought a glorious calm over me. Although you may try, you cannot always control the things that happen to you or the world around you. The one thing you can control is how your mind perceives things. You can learn to control your ability to see them as both positive and negative so that you can better adapt.

You must appreciate your strengths as well as your weaknesses. Learn to accept life, and do your best to blend with it. However good or bad a situation is, it is both, and it will also change.

Let's continue this train of thought to see more of this law of yin and yang. Our brain has two sides. One side (left) absorbs and interprets words, numbers, the linear, and so on—basic logical things. The other side (right), interprets pictures, color, concepts—emotional, intuitive, creative, and spiritual things.

Electricity has negative and positive poles, as do magnets that we find in the earth. When we move, one muscle tightens and contracts while the opposing one relaxes and stretches. Our eyes allow us to see a central field of vision (direct viewpoint) as well as peripheral views to either side of us. When we breathe, we inhale oxygen and exhale carbon dioxide—trees and plants around us take in carbon dioxide and give us back pure oxygen. This is the harmony found in nature.

It's interesting to note that you can't start your car if the battery cable is connected to only the positive. You also have to connect the negative cable. Life is constantly yin and yang. We must learn to take the good along with the bad. A most important maxim states: "There is no disaster that can't become a blessing, and no blessing that can't become a disaster."

People refer to karma as destiny but, in fact, the word actually translates as "action and reaction." Traditional Buddhist law of dependent origination means that every cause has an effect and that every effect has a cause. The master understands the death of a caterpillar is the birth of a butterfly. Be the master of your life.

As you accept these facts, you can appreciate that any situation—physical, mental, or emotional—is subject to the yin and yang. Just as we realize that we cannot control either side, we understand that we need to embrace who we are by accepting the situation and blending with it. Problems and fear will overwhelm you when you fight them. But they can also be a beneficial and a necessary ally. By accepting the situation, you can become one with it and get through it. We will discuss how to use and appreciate life's negative as well as positive experiences—and how to use them to your advantage.

As you embark across the two-by-four of your life, focus on walking it and not on the fear of falling or failing. Be in the moment.

The more you understand and are in harmony with your own mind and body, the more you can be in harmony with the things around you. This is not necessarily to control but to better understand how to adapt to the situation or better appreciate or accept the circumstance. To be in harmony with yourself as well as those around you is the first step to conquering any obstacle. The foundation to inner peace and true enlightenment is to accept that everyone and everything are interdependent. You must emotionalize and practice these concepts.

This balance we all need relates to your life in numerous ways. From the need to balance your budget or diet to balancing your emotions, you must consider two sides to every decision. In the following chapters, you will find how this balance applies to all types of situations and how you can flow with life's many challenges by blending with—and not fighting— the circumstances you will encounter. Now that you are becoming more familiar with the yin and yang principles, let's discuss how they apply to you, your life, and the choices you make.

Important Bullet Points

1. Realize that there are two sides to every story.
2. Try to see the yin and yang in all things so as to not make one-sided choices.
3. Be your own devil's advocate or seek out another point of view.
4. Accept the situation you are in as both good and bad, and see how you can blend with it.
5. Your struggle or fear is both big and small and good and bad, depending on what you are comparing it to and how you approach it.
6. The way you see yourself is who you are. You are in control of your point of view.
7. There are things you don't have that someone else has, but there are things you have that someone else lacks.
8. The water that can take you to the bottom and drown you is the same water you need to swim to the top.
9. Don't wait to fall in the water before you learn how to swim. Be proactive.
10. Balancing the opposites that affect your life is important.
11. Everything difficult is also simple once you accept and understand it.
12. By improving yourself, you help others, and by helping others, you improve yourself.
13. Break down your fears and problems to help you overcome them.
14. Everything is different and the same. Use what you know to help you understand what you don't know.
15. Your pain, suffering, and obstacles will benefit you or may be to help others. We are all interdependent.

16. Tap into your strengths as well as your weaknesses, as they both serve a purpose.
17. The good or bad of any situation you face depends on your perspective, and your perspective depends on you.
18. Failure and pain are a necessary part of your successes and pleasures.
19. Everything in your life is as important as it is insignificant.
20. Be in the moment.

CHAPTER TWO

POWER THOUGHTS

Bert Rodriguez

Motivation Fuel

We constantly need motivation. Motivation fuels the fire that burns inside you. It forges you as well as the weapons you must have to conquer and overcome your challenges. You have to feed and stoke your fire every day or it will cool down and die. The fire you need to create yourself into the warrior you must be will die along with it! Keep those fires burning.

A Paragon of Life

All things in nature (as well as our lives) are a constant interplay of violent chaos and calm tranquility—yin and yang. We must realize and accept that on the calmest day, in the most tranquil moment, a storm-like disruption and disorder can suddenly appear; we must learn to maintain an inward peace and a clear mind while in the midst of turmoil.

To be at one with this law of yin and yang that is part of all things is necessary to live and enjoy a happy, productive and successful existence.

The Power of Love

Love is a powerful emotion. It transcends what the eyes see; what the mind thinks.

Love is a force usually associated with a bond that connects us to our loved ones or even our pets, but it is a force which can also be applied to your goals, dreams, or aspirations. When you commit your heart and soul to what you want to achieve in life, the feeling of love and passion will fuel you and keep you on course. Love empowers you to conquer, transcend, and defeat obstacles or fears that may get in the way of all that you can manifest in your life. Love yourself first so you can then share and use this force that is part of life in a positive way.

Envision what you seek. Commit to this goal and give it your love and passion. Never waver or let your resolve grow weary and you will reach success.

Choices and Decisions

Life is a constant road of confrontations with choices and decisions. Making tough decisions can be stressful and consuming. You must find the courage to take a leap of faith— even when the consequences may seem vague or unknown. Fear and doubt will keep you in a frozen catatonic state. By not making a decision and bravely accepting responsibility for whatever the outcome, you will guarantee certain failure. You will never discover what could have been. Live life to the fullest or die trying.

Bert Rodriguez

Success in Failure

If you can accept and appreciate the duality of life—the positive and negative aspect of every incident and occurrence you experience—you will see that even in failure there is success.

The Product of Your Thoughts

We are not subject or slaves to our circumstances and environment. Everything you have accomplished, acquired, and experienced as well as everything you have failed at, lost, and suffered through were a product of your thoughts and daily behavior. Your deepest thoughts and beliefs can, do, and will create your circumstances and mold your environment.

You possess the ability to master your thoughts and beliefs. Whatever you create in your mind, think of consistently, hold true to in your heart, and follow up with your actions will manifest itself in your life.

Your Existence

Take time to re-evaluate your daily existence. Not what you do but the why you do it. If your motives are not emotionally driven toward helping someone or something greater than yourself, your life will begin to feel empty and meaningless.

Your Real Challenge

Those who train or workout for fitness, health benefits, fun, or to compete in any sport or athletic activity, realize that you don't do it necessarily to be perfect, look like an Adonis, or be a world champion! The value is in learning about commitment, courage, discipline, endurance, dedication, and determination—face adversity; endure pain, loss, failure; and still not give up.

To conquer yourself, your fears, and overcome the real challenges you face, stay on course. Realize and appreciate the true meaning and value of your efforts.

Developing Real Power

We strive to be stronger individuals. We all consciously or unconsciously crave and want power. We also don't like to feel others have power over us. We want to overpower the competition in school, sports, games, or with adversaries of any kind—in conversations or in other encounters. We want to feel like winners, not losers.

Sometimes we fail to realize how internal power can trump our physical power. We may execute this power through our roles as leaders, parents, or employers or in other relationships. We may use our internal and emotional power by controlling or restricting favors, compliments, friendship, love, forgiveness, or even conversation. Sometimes, we try to assert our power over others with material things like money, shelter, food, clothing, and other objects.

This can turn our daily existence into a constant struggle with our minds as well as with family, friends, and strangers. We don't want to relinquish power. We often feel that by empowering others we give them power over us, but the truth is: the more you empower others, the more powerful you become. Giving yourself or others one minute to lift the spirit and help them discover their own strengths is worth more than years of denying it because of ego, resentment, revenge, or guilt.

Measure your personal power not by how much you have over others but by how much you have over yourself. Don't keep yourself from developing real power.

You Will Reap What You Sow

Sometimes we keep from giving or sharing what we have with others because we feel lacking in our own lives. We do this with material things as well as spiritually when we fail to give someone a compliment, a kind word, support, love, or forgiveness. We do not all share the same weaknesses or have needs in the same areas. You will find that by helping someone fill their need, they can in turn help you fill yours.

Enthusiastic Passion

Although you may not always win, it's good to have a game plan. Your odds of success greatly improve if you know what you need to start. Enthusiasm and passion should be at the top of your list.

Selling Yourself

There is one rule of thumb that has made the top salesperson in any field successful: If you don't believe in your product, you will not be successful at selling it.

You may not realize it, but from the time you were a child you have had a job. This job has been to sell yourself. If you've had a hard time getting a career, building relationships, or reaching your goals, this may very well be what has held you back. Belief in your "self" is what makes the asset that you are truly valuable.

Lack or Abundance

To be in a state of mind where you think you have been shortchanged or are lacking the things that you feel could make you happy in life is only creating a situation that will not help you acquire what you need or want to manifest in your life. It is a negative mindset you have created by an incorrect comparison.

 Take the time to value and be grateful for the things you have and you will see the abundance what others would give anything to possess. This will replace your thoughts with a positive outlook of appreciating and realizing all that you have already achieved or gained and that you are well on your way to bigger and greater things.

Your Destiny

Sometimes we need to make adjustments on our journey to our purpose. Few of us are willing to make radical changes in our lives. Fate is how your life unfolds when you let fear or doubt determine your choices or say, "Let's see what happens." The destiny that you can create will reveal itself to you when you confront your fears and make a conscious choice to "make things happen."

Always making the best of a bad situation will empower your future. This is how balancing the law of opposites works.

Energy

Everything in our universe is pure energy—both negative and positive—from atoms that are made up of neutrons and protons to magnets and electricity (which we benefit from daily). Our physical energy cannot be seen, but it is there. We may not realize, but it emanates from us and affects the things around us, including each other.

This force we possess and are all part of can be both constructive and destructive. It can be used to build or destroy tangible structures as well as intangible (mental and emotional) ones, like loving relationships, circumstances, opportunities, and friendships. Love, caring, forgiveness, and compassion make up one half of the energy field. Hatred, indifference, revenge, and lack of sympathy make up the other half.

What you hold within your heart and mind permeates and exudes from you to your demeanor as well as to your physical countenance. Learn to seek out and tap into the good things in your life. You will always reflect who you truly are. Spread the joy and smile more often. It will result in your living a more fruitful and happy existence.

Getting Past Fear

There are four ways you can handle fear. You can go around it. You can go over it. You can go under it, but if you ever want to conquer it, you must face it, grab it, look it in the eye in order to control it and overcome it.

Creating Character

You are, daily, creating your character. This is the foundation of who you are and who you will be in the future. You are doing it by what you think, what you see, what you hear, what you say, and what you do; what moves you mentally and spiritually, what inspires you, what you have passion for, and the philosophy you live by. These are the building blocks of character that will lead you to greatness.

Encourage Someone

From early childhood, we crave and seek support, accolades, and recognition from our mothers and fathers, as well as from those we respect and look up to. Any trophy, blue ribbon, certificate, or degree that declares achievement gives us motivation to rise to a higher level; it empowers us to go further. Take the time to encourage someone today. You may be just what they need to lift them to their highest potential.

Life's Pain and Pleasure

The first truth in Buddhism is that life is suffering. When combined with the truth of impermanence and the harmony between opposites, it makes perfect sense. If today you began a regimen to improve your flexibility, muscle tone, or skill in any activity you would immediately experience discomfort and feel some pain. Tomorrow you would surely feel stiff as well as sore.

This is one part of the process. If you cower, back off, or quit, you will never achieve your goal. If you endure, work through it, and continue moving towards your quest, those feelings will soon pass, and you will arrive at your new comfort level.

Once again you must step out of your comfort zone and repeat the same process to rise to the next highest level. This is the irony and balance of life. You can't enjoy the pleasure without accepting the pain. This is the truth with any achievement or success.

Go With the Flow

Don't let what may seem like negative situations overwhelm you or keep you down. Let things flow and follow their natural course. Cold creates a desire for warmth, weakness a need for strength, loss a need to find, hunger a desire for food, poverty a desire for riches. Negatives can turn into positives. Let your needs and desires motivate and fuel your achievements.

Your Biggest Battle

Who will be your next opponent? Who will you battle in your next big fight? There are two strengths we need to develop and two battles we must all face: physical and mental. When was the last time you were in a physical fight? Yet both physically and mentally you have one every day of your life. The physical opponent the majority of us encounter won't be another person. It will be your own body and your ability to control it in the myriad activities you perform every day—things you might do at work or home, in sports, in your workouts, having fun, or just daily tasks.

The greater majority of the mental battles will also be with yourself—your own thoughts, emotions, and the decisions that you have to make on a minute-to-minute basis. The battles that will include other people will also not be against punches, kicks, or weapons, but instead come in the form of words, situations, and circumstances.

The truth is that you really don't want to have to fight. You actually want to blend. With any situation, fighting leads to struggling and possible defeat. Blending gives you a better chance to be in harmony with as well as control and succeed in your purpose—which should obviously be to not lose, fail, or be overwhelmed by whatever situation you may face.

In any battle, the ability to use the opposing force against itself and in your favor is the main key to success. All of life is about blending with the forces found in nature or with circumstances in order to come out unscathed or victorious. We must learn to be in harmony with ourselves, others, and life. The true study of martial arts is not about fighting but about self-control, both physically and mentally. The more you can control yourself, the better you will control any situation. Mentally, this includes your control of fear, doubt, anger, ego, and your other emotions. Fighting is not the way to achieve success in all the things you will encounter in life. Being in harmony is the way to true success.

"It is not the most intellectual of the species that survives; it is not the strongest that survives; but the species that survives is the one that is able to adapt to and to adjust best to the changing environment in which it finds itself."[1]

---

[1]   While this quote has been often attributed to Origin of Species by Charles Darwin, it has been noted that it is actually a paraphrased quote from said work and is attributed to Leon C. Megginson, "Lessons from Europe for American Business," Southwestern Social Science Quarterly, 44/1 (1963): 3-13, quote at 4

Bert Rodriguez

The Power of Belief

There is a power that can be found in the form of an unshakable, subconscious, deep-seeded belief. Belief works as an invisible spirit within you that can make miracles happen in your life in ways that can only be explained as unlikely or impossible.

No Destination

There is no such thing as a destination. Your life is an endless, ongoing, adventurous journey. You exist as who you are at this moment, but who you were or who will become is not in your grasp. You are constantly evolving and becoming.

Bert Rodriguez

When Fear Controls You

When fear controls your will, nothing can be accomplished. It is the loss of nerve, determination, intensity of purpose, and the courage to at least try that makes you a coward and will guarantee certain failure.

Your Strengths

The strengths you possess—both mentally and physically—are unbelievable. The mind is where they are stored. Your ability to tap into your subconscious power is the secret.

When you find yourself in a dangerous situation, faced with an emergency, competing, working out, trying to take yourself to the next level, or just trying to win or achieve your goal, the mental focus of your subconscious and body harmony is what can get you there. Your conscious mind wants it, and you say to yourself "I'm doing this"—but this is also the part of the brain that harbors your doubts.

It is these doubts that negate your ability to overcome your obstacle. Having strong desires but also having strong doubts means your desire will not become a reality. It is your subconscious mind that houses the triggers that can give you the strength to make it happen. I relate in my book Face Fear, Create Courage how someone in an emotional, hypnotic state can get stabbed, shot, burned, or lose a limb and still continue. A person can overcome odds that would stop them in their tracks under normal conditions, but the emotion and the true heartfelt desire to save a child, a loved one, or even to save themselves can give you super-human strengths. The fact that there is no doubt that you will survive and overcome the challenge in front of you is what makes it possible.

Although this may sound silly, when I would tire on a run, I would visualize and convince myself that my house was burning down and I had to get there to save my son.

This focus on this self-hypnotizing, visual mindset would make me overcome any pain or thoughts of quitting, slowing down, or giving up. In fact, I would feel a surge of strength come over me from the adrenaline and chemicals released from my body's stores.

Work on and practice the ability to use these and not let this doubt interfere with their release and your performance. Doubt will destroy any chance you have to accomplish what you are trying to do. Visualize and feel that you need to lift that weight, pull your body up, or accomplish your chosen goal for the sake of something that is of greater importance and purpose to you than just trying to outdo yourself or win a competitive event. Tell yourself that you cannot and will not fail. You will marvel at the capabilities that are at your disposal.

Be Resilient

Unpleasant moments will definitely be a part of life. We need to be resilient. Webster defines "resiliency" as "the ability to recover quickly from an illness, change, or misfortune; buoyancy." Go with the flow and be in harmony with yourself and the circumstances that confront you. Bounce back with more resolve and level of commitment and conquer the moment.

Change

Nothing is. All things are constantly changing. You are "nothing," wu-shih.

Your concept of who you are is developed by your experiences and your response to them. It is not a label or any other description of you that defines your total self. But your self-concept of who you are can greatly influence who or what you will become. You are not a "thing" but a "process" that is continuously open to change. Flow and grow with the power of your creative thoughts.

Perfection

Your fear of not being the perfect you that you should be and are striving to become can be disheartening. It can stop you in your tracks and keep you from attaining your vision of being in shape, having the perfect body, feeling totally qualified in any area, or conquering your challenge.

You will never be perfect! It is an imaginary quest and goal. It is a road you must travel in the now, full of obstacles and mistakes that are inevitable when you are on it. That is the only path you can take to get closer to reaching your destination. But it never ends because perfection is never attainable or real. The road is real, the journey is real, the obstacles are real, the mistakes are real, the hard work and pain are real, and it is what the road you are on is made of. The more you travel on it, the happier and more content you are with yourself, where you are, and what you have already achieved. When you have the body, the goal, or whatever other vision you were heading to, you will need to replace it with another. Because it is a never-ending road! It is your expectations that create you and the world around you. Now that you have decided to travel it, enjoy the journey and all the ups and downs you will encounter.

Visualize Your Journey

You will navigate and head in the direction of what you visualize and expect in your life, whether you expect good things or bad. See yourself and expect good health, prosperity, and success. See yourself reaching your goal. Envision what you are striving for. You must look for and get ready for good things and be prepared before you get them.

If you don't at least expect something to happen, you will surely never reach your goals. You should always believe and have expectancy for the great things that are going to happen in your life.

The Force That Is Thought

Everything you see around you on this earth was a thought first. Your thoughts are powerful and you can turn them into reality. First you must see, create, and picture them in your mind. Next you must believe in the power and in yourself. And finally you must connect with and use the power given to you by The Force.

Life Is a Joke

I love to laugh. I like a good joke and I love to share a good joke with friends or family. We all do. It's great to make someone else laugh and be happy. The trouble is I'm not a comedian, although I have occasionally come up with a funny comment or even by chance put together a good joke.

The good jokes that have made me laugh, the ones that I share, I usually got from someone else who did or said something funny. The best jokes I have heard have been from professional comedians. Good comedians are always trying to get new ideas and material, sometimes consulting with other writers, even though they have told many good jokes and have been successful at it.

If you want to get good advice on any subject (sports, training, nutrition, business, comedy, etc.) or learn how to do something efficiently, go to someone with experience in that area. At this moment, I'm on a new business venture—actually a couple of different ones. I want to succeed, so I ask anyone I know in business all sorts of questions. People also ask me about the same.

What I share, and what has worked for me, I probably learned from someone else. I don't make it up, just like I don't make up jokes that have made me laugh and that I share. The information comes from something I have picked up from experience and failures or from others.

If you want to succeed at whatever you want to venture into, save yourself time, effort, and the risk of failure and disappointment by seeking out ideas, advice, and suggestions from those who know.

We are all interdependent and will learn as well as teach in life. You will always be in a position where someone knows something you don't and vice versa! Appreciate that very important yin and yang of life and you will fare much better. You will encourage others as well as need others to encourage you. Know when to listen, and you will know when to speak.

Your GPS

It would be convenient to have a perfectly laid out map or instructions that would guide you to your goals in life. Actually you are already factory-equipped with what you need. To accomplish and reach your dreams and plans, you must use your mind like the GPS in your car—the road to success can be traveled with certainty by using this natural GPS. First you must know exactly where you are and exactly where you want to be. Most people fail to reach their destination, not because they lack the ability or don't possess the natural attributes, but because they fail to listen to that little voice, their own intuition. They let doubt lead the way and fail to use this guiding system, trust it and believe you will arrive at your chosen destination.

First You Must Believe

We have all heard the sayings "I'll believe it when I see it" or "seeing is believing." They are both not true!

Actually, it's the opposite. Believing is seeing. You have to believe it in order to see it! Were this not so, every great invention, advancement, and creation you see on this earth today (and that we use, enjoy, and benefit from) would not have come into reality. The men that created them did so first in their thoughts, combining that with a strong "belief" it was possible.

In every case, they faced critics, skeptics, and doubters. But their strong belief and conviction is what they used to not give up on their vision. Never doubt yourself, your potential, or ability to succeed or accomplish anything your mind creates or your heart desires. Remember that everything you see on this earth was a thought first.

A Dark Place

Be one with the moments when your life is at a low point or you experience a dark state of mind. Accept and learn to be at one with your hardest and most painful experiences.

When you find yourself in a dark place, see it as being in a maze that has an entrance and an exit. If you look at it only with your eyes and what is directly in front of you at the moment, you see only darkness and fear. Look at it with your heart and mind and think: It is up to me whether it's a chamber of darkness that I can't escape or a tunnel to the light of a new day. This will help create your strength of character and help you appreciate and get through the maze of dark and light that is an inevitable part of life.

Take Time to Meditate

Meditation should be part of your everyday life. Through meditation, you observe yourself. It helps you experience serenity. We create our experiences by the activity of our thinking.

Everything in the manifest realm had its beginning in thought. You need serenity to take control of your emotions. Exercise, as well as nutritional discipline, can be used as systems of meditation because it takes discipline to wrestle and control mind and body into a place where it is quiet and serene.

It will help you learn to center the mind. It is how you can receive answers to who you are, your purpose, and the interdependent nature of your reality. Meditation or prayer is creative thinking that heightens the connection with a universal intelligence and divine spirit that is part of us all. It, therefore, encompasses positive energy that brings forth wisdom, healing, prosperity, and everything good.

The River of Life

The journey to reach your goal or purpose in life involves flowing steadily down a river that you must travel in order to arrive at your destination. At times, it will be pleasant and serene but you will inevitably encounter some strong currents and rough waters. It can be an exciting adventure and an enjoyable ride if you let it take you with its own force to all the strange new shores, circumstances, places, and people you will meet. The more you struggle to control or fight the current, the harder your journey will become and the longer it will take you to reach your destination.

When you feel the pull of an inconvenience or difficult situation, you must flow with it and be in the now. Be one with what you are doing and where you are at the moment. The lesson you learn and what you are experiencing is part of the trip and will help you appreciate and enjoy the destination that much more.

Never lose the vision of what you are trying to achieve but remember that the journey is an integral and the most important part of reaching any goal. The ability to blend with and be in harmony with every aspect of life is empowering, refreshing, and releasing.

Courage

To achieve real success in anything you choose, you must have the courage to take risk. What others may perceive as impulsive or even reckless can be essential.

Playing it safe can sometimes slow you down, keep you from taking advantage of opportunities, or just keep you from ever taking that important first step. The fear of the unknown has thwarted many achievements. Believe in yourself. Have the confidence to trust your ability to conquer any obstacle you may encounter. I have used this formula to go beyond my natural capabilities, talent, and potential. You can, too. Be fearless. The main obstacle to overcoming any of the problems you may face is not having the courage to challenge them.

Bert Rodriguez

May the Force Be with You

"The Force," referred to in Star Wars, is real and all around you in everything you see. It makes the world go round. It gives you life. "The force is with you" but you have to acknowledge, understand, and believe in it in order to tap into and use its energy.

May the Force be with you.

Take a Bite

"The way to eat an elephant, is one bite at a time."

Years of thinking about your goals are not worth the one day when you take the first steps toward achieving them. Have the courage to take action or you'll live your life as only a dreamer. Take that first bite!

Bert Rodriguez

What Are You Lacking?

Failure in the attempt to reach any goal can be pinned on what you're lacking. It may be a lack of willpower; a lack of purpose or courage; a lack of commitment or responsibility; a tendency to give up at the first sign of hardship; a lack of self-confidence or enthusiasm; an inability to control emotions; laziness; narrow-mindedness; a lack of creativity and self-control. Some people may fail to reach a goal because they expect a lot from others but are not willing to give of themselves; some will live a lie instead of admitting they are wrong.

This is an epidemic that is affecting us today and will destroy our advancements as individuals and as a society. We have to face reality and take responsibility for our actions and our personal lives. Never stop taking those steps to self-improvement. You have everything you need and the ability to create a better you. Do it, for yourself, for those you love, and to know in your heart that you gave it your very best and never gave up.

The Power That Is Spirit

There isn't one of us that at times doesn't feel down, defeated, hopeless, or dispirited. To be in good spirits or inspired is associated with an overall good feeling of commitment, courage, and a tenacious "go for it" attitude. Your spirit is an unseen power and is the connection between your thoughts and your physical being. It is what fuels the sensation of being alive—of having purpose and a final goal. Without it we feel empty and dead.

Find something that emotionally moves and inspires you. Chase it; hold on to it. Give it all you've got. This is the greatest secret to enjoying life.

Bert Rodriguez

Peace of Mind

If you want tranquility and peace of mind in your life, stop the struggle within yourself. When you resent, resist, dislike, or fight what you must do or the situations you find yourself in, you are creating an opponent.

Overwhelmed

Is your journey in your search for self-improvement, for self-empowerment, sometimes overwhelming? As you strive to create the best version of you in your life, for yourself as well as for those you care for, do you feel alone?

We are all in a constant struggle to live up to the expectations we have of ourselves. We are trying to accomplish the dreams and plans we had and shared from childhood with our friends, classmates, family, teachers, and those that wanted to see us succeed as well as those who wanted to see us fail.

Although we all have different goals with what we feel will bring us happiness and contentment, we are all on the same road trying to reach the same destination. To win, to overcome! Life, nature, and the way of Zen teach us that we are all interdependent. Even when it seems that you are competing against others as well as circumstances you confront, you need these to rise to your highest potential. Accept, appreciate, respect your opposition as well as the challenges and obstacles you encounter.

You could never make it without them. You are never alone!

Fighting Yourself

The majority of us rarely, if ever, get into a physical fight or face real death. Yet mentally, we are daily in constant battle. Our ego, pride, and self-esteem are afraid of the death of who we think we are or of losing to circumstances, arguments, or situations.

The fear of failure, loss, or being wrong is where we feel threatened and what confronts us every day. Our ego can be our greatest opponent. This is why we fight with friends, in relationships, and wars that are being fought around the world this very moment.

Once we understand the principles of yin and yang, we realize we will be right only 50 percent of the time. Accepting this will help us lead a more calm and peaceful existence within ourselves. It will in turn let us deal more intelligently with the outside world and the real obstacles we must face.

What You Resist Persists

One of the realities of life and a basic premise in metaphysics is that "what you resist persists." It could be physical as well as mental. It could be the loss of your money, your job, your home, a family member, a relationship, or even a simple competition.

Stop fighting or resisting the circumstances of failure and loss that is inevitable in life. We try to fight back with weapons of anger, sadness, and frustration, but our resistance keeps everything in place and in front of us. It also keeps us from facing and working on trying to accept and deal with the things we know we could certainly overcome.

Let life throw whatever it wants at you. Face and confront your worst fears. You may feel discomfort or sensations that may be troubling—just like the pain and the black eye you might get when you stand up to a bully—but facing your battles is the only way to win. Running, ignoring, or hiding from them never works. Use the negative side of the yin and yang as a catalyst that fuels your ability to conquer the world.

Face your fear to create courage.

Bert Rodriguez

Karma

One of the main laws of physics is that to every action there is an equal and opposite reaction. Your success, reward, or what you get from (or out) of any experience is equal to what you offer and the effort that you put into the experience.

Your life is the product of the combination of your mind, your speech, and your actions. What you can imagine, your thoughts, what you say, and the actions you take will create your circumstances. They will also be the catalyst for what you get back in return.

Being Judgmental

It's ironic that when judging the behavior of others we compare our good qualities and virtues with their faults and shortcomings—never the other way around. This puts us at a disadvantage when accessing and maintaining friendships and relationships. Learn to understand and work with the good and the bad characteristics about yourself as well as those of others. We are none of us perfect.

Who's Fault Is It?

When dealing with others and difficulties or adversities arise—at work, in friendships, business, or romantic relationships—we immediately think that the other person is being unreasonable, crazy, or they need to change. We either try to convince them they're wrong (or try to change them) or walk away only to find the same circumstances elsewhere. This is like looking in the mirror, not liking what you see and going to another mirror hoping to see something different reflected there.

This is what happens when we fail to acknowledge that all of life is a reflection of our own thoughts and actions. We each create our own reality as well as life's circumstances. If this were not so, we would be living the opposite and all be puppets with our strings being pulled and controlled by others. But we are not puppets! You—and only you—are in charge of your life and the events you are subjected to. Stop blaming others for what you are fully responsible for! Be honest enough with yourself and take the credit for your achievements as well as your failures.

Be Fearless

Do you want to be totally fearless? Never, ever be afraid again—of anything? Here's how. If you want to overcome any fear you have of doing anything you want, whether it's to compete in a sport, get on stage, say something to someone, take on a new challenge, start a new business, quit a job, move to a new place, fall in love, or anything else, the way to do it is to accept the feelings that come with it. This is the yin and yang of every situation. That's what you're afraid of. It's not succeeding or the event you're afraid of, it's the feeling or emotional sensation that comes along with it if you fail—the hurt, pain, disappointment. And that is an unavoidable part of the equation.

Fighting is a good analogy. Everybody thinks a fighter is not afraid to fight, to get in the ring, get hit (or that getting hit doesn't hurt). The fighter is afraid, it does hurt to get hit, and there are the worries that any performer might experience— like looking bad or losing. The big difference is that his desire to win, to succeed, to feel the rush of being on top, to overcome the challenge, is greater than the pain or fear of anything else that may occur.

Being totally at one with and accepting the inevitable two sides, the inherent negative as well as positive in all things, makes you the master of your life. Being willing to die makes you enjoy and love life. Cowards die a thousand deaths; heroes, only once.

Someday

Never wait for "someday" or "some other time" or a special occasion to do something with or say something to someone. Every day can be that "someday" and be the perfect day to start your quest. You may never get a second chance.

Be in the Now

Zen teaches us to be in the Now, a way of focusing or being in the zone. Great artist, athletes, musicians, craftsmen, and others, achieve this state of mind when performing. You can use this to improve your own performance in whatever you choose. You can practice this next time you are doing any routine activity like brushing your teeth, washing your hands, walking up or down stairs, or anything else. Observe every little detail: the sound of the water, your breathing, your every intricate movement. Pay attention to all of your senses. Notice the feeling of calm and concentrated focus you begin to achieve. Become aware of your sense of presence. You will feel yourself getting better at it. Then try it next time you're doing something that requires your full attention, calmness, concentration, and full mind-body synchronization. When you're losing your cool in traffic, work, or any other frustrating situation: Breath. Stay calm. Life will be a joyful adventure.

Meditation

Meditation or serene quiet focus induces creative thinking that heightens the connection with all of nature and the world around you. You become part universal intelligence and divine spirit that is part of all things. It, therefore, encompasses positive energy that brings you to a place of total peace and contentment.

Flow Like Water

As we find ourselves confronting the struggles we face in life, we often ask, "How can I get this situation under control?" Life is not about control. It is about acquiring the ability to blend, to flow like water does with anything that stands in its way. We have to do the same with the challenges, obstacles, and problems that threaten to stop our path and the current of growth and progress with which we are flowing. Be soft and pliable like water and you will wash through, flow over and around, and then past your hardest moments.

Inspire Others

Be creative in finding ways to make your life and purpose in this world more valuable. Find more, as well as better, ways to be an inspiration and encouragement to as many people as you can. Increase both the quality and the quantity.

You will discover that nothing is more rewarding and pays higher dividends than giving of yourself to help or lift up the spirits of someone in need.

When Fear Controls You

When fear controls your will, nothing can be accomplished. It is this weakening of willpower, nerve, determination, intensity of purpose, and the courage to try that makes you catatonic and keeps you from moving forward.

Your Credibility

Your words can create positive as well as negative effects and situations in your life. To be impeccable with your word gives you credibility.

The word "credit" derives from the word credibility. To have credibility gives you power. It says in the Bible that God spoke a word and created everything we see. This is where the word "universe" comes from; it translates to "one verse."

You create your world, your personal universe, with what you think and the words you speak. Be true to your words, to yourself, and to others. Use your words wisely; they are valuable tools that you will use to build your life, your future, and your successes as well as your failures.

Once You Make Up Your Mind

We've all heard the expression "once I make my mind up" and yet we fail to see that our mind and the thoughts we nurture in it is what makes things happen in our lives. Sometimes we unconsciously (and yet deliberately) put ourselves in situations or fail because we can't make up our minds or by harboring thoughts that become detrimental to our forward progress.

Desperate moments can bring out the true strength that is in you. Just as a drowning man will either give up or do his best and struggle to reach for anything he can to save himself or a starving man will eat scraps or whatever is available in order to live, the minute we conquer our fears and we "make up our mind" to overcome, survive, and succeed, we seem to draw on a power that is within all of us that can help us conquer any obstacle and accomplish anything we desire.

All your successes have been fueled by this power and preceded by what may have seemed like a negative moment in your life. Sometimes we have to step in something that could soil or permanently damage our shoes in order to motivate us to clean them up or get a new pair. All we need to do have faith that once we make up our mind, we will accomplish anything we truly and totally commit to with every fiber of our being.

We are the creators of this experience that is life.

Bert Rodriguez

You Are a Walking Billboard

We are all walking billboards. Your thoughts are creating what others see. They will observe, interpret, and judge you by what you display. What you think will show itself, not just in your actions but also in the way you look, your attire, body movements, facial expressions, and especially your eyes.

Look around, study yourself and those you associate with at work, on the street, or wherever you go. Look closely and you can see a person's character. You can see who has the potential to succeed in life and who will probably fail.

Who has the intensity of purpose and who will just coast with the circumstances? Be true to yourself and take care that your thoughts create exactly what you want to show the world you represent, who you really are, and who you strive to be.

The Answer

Everything you want or need to know and the knowledge of how to manifest or achieve it is within your grasp. We are all connected to a database of human consciousness that is the realm of genius. You are part of this universal, common consciousness that we all share. You must shut off the chatter that occupies your mind and thoughts to be able to tap into and listen to what it can reveal to you.

Slow down, let your mind be silent, in this introspecting peace and through meditation you will discover the answers and learn more than you could ever imagine.

The Eye of the Storm

It's interesting to note that in the great forces of nature—found in the wind and water, in hurricanes and tornadoes—as devastating and destructive as the turmoil and chaos of its outside can be, its center remains in a state of calmness and tranquility. Just as there is calm at the center of these powerful forces, the individual that remains the most at ease in any situation is the one in control and has the greatest strength to tear through and overcome any obstacle in their path.

Nature is about balance, a force that can destroy can also create. Having a peaceful and tranquil mind brings confidence, energy, and power. Realizing this will help you appreciate and accept that within you lies a force that can help you bring forth and manifest everything you wish and want your life to be. It can be positive or negative, beneficial or detrimental. If you see yourself as weak or unable and that nothing great or exciting will happen then this is what you will experience. If you believe in your abilities and in the power and energy that lies within you, then all things become a possibility. A calm mind, as well as a few moments of daily quiet and peaceful meditation, can tremendously strengthen your resolve. Be in harmony with and control the forces of your storms.

Your Plans

Setting a goal without creating, developing, and following a solid plan is like using a plastic knife to cut the wood you need to build a fire. To successfully achieve your goals, you need strong tools in the form of an efficient plan.

Although you may not always succeed, your chances of reaching your goal will increase. Then your commitment, enthusiasm, passion, and diligence in following your plan will help you accomplish your goals.

Bert Rodriguez

Life Is a Mirror

Life is a reflection, a mirror of what you put in front of it. You can't expect to see a reflection of yourself in fancy clothes if you go around wearing rags. You can't expect to get a smile if you only give people a frown. You can't expect for people to treat you fairly if you treat others unfairly. You can't expect success without projecting the effort by going out and working for it. You can't expect a rose to grow in your garden without taking all the necessary steps and putting in the time it takes to help it bloom. You can't do a good deed without having one done to you in return. To have an honest, meaningful friendship or relationship, you must be willing to sincerely give one.

We all want, but when it comes time to give, we fail to pay for what we desire and ask for. If you want to bear and enjoy the taste of the fruit tomorrow, you must plant the seed and nurture it today. Experience it for yourself. The next time you go out, speak and act as if you're upset and note the reaction you receive. Try it again with a friendly attitude and a smile and observe the difference. That is the way of life; you will get back everything that you project outwardly, be it positive or negative.

You Can Lead or Follow

Are you a leader or a follower? Both have value. The follower enjoys the comfort of not having to make decisions, stress out, think, plan, or be held responsible if things go amiss. The leader enjoys the thrill of turning thoughts into reality, as well as the adventure, creativity, and planning that go along with it. She glows with the feeling of the joy, pleasure, and self-satisfaction when she succeeds.

Which do you prefer? If you don't create and follow your own thoughts and dreams, you will follow the people who created and followed theirs.

Bert Rodriguez

Winning or Losing with Your Attitude

People often remark that I seem to come out ahead or end up winning in situations and circumstances that appeared to be stacked against me. They ask me how this is possible. One person remarked how it seemed that throughout my life, even when I stepped in crap, I came up smelling like a rose.

Every situation has the potential of being negative or positive. Wherever I find myself, my mind searches for how what is happening could be beneficial or a positive for me. I always try my best to seek out and project positive even in the negative, not only towards myself but especially towards others. Even in the worst times of my life, when I was on the streets, struggling to survive, I always looked for the positive side of the situation. I treated everyone fairly and tried to help everyone I could.

The more you reach out, encourage, motivate, inspire, and empower others to overcome their challenges, the more those same attributes will come back to you. It seems I have created a situation where there's always a line of people ready and willing to help me. You can harvest the same things in your life. Don't let what may seem like negative people or situations overwhelm you or keep you down. Maintain a strong winning attitude towards whatever you confront.

Coincidence?

What may appear as coincidences may not be coincidences at all but simply the working out of a pattern that you started and are experiencing with your own mind and thoughts.

Bert Rodriguez

Do You Believe?

There is a powerful force that can be found in unshakable, deep-seated belief. Belief works as an invisible spirit within you that can make things, which can only be explained as unbelievable or miracles, happen in your life.

Keep an Open Mind

Throughout the history of man's existence and progress, we have often times been our own worst enemy. Our closed-minded attitudes, prejudice opinions, and stubbornness against accepting new ideas and concepts have kept us from advancing 100 times more rapidly than we have.

Every great scientist, inventor, and innovator has been either persecuted or afraid to come out with new ideas or innovations because they would be ridiculed, laughed at, or even burned at the stake. The established powers or knowledge did not want to be challenged or lose their perceived advantage of knowing more than the rest. These fools—thinking that their persecution of new ideas, information or opinions gave them superiority—restrained innovation and advancement. Science, medicine, politics, and even religion remained frozen in time until irrefutable proof showed their folly and ignorance—and often there was still a refusal to accept they were wrong.

This way of thinking has not changed. We were meant to evolve, to grow, and to improve daily—physically, mentally, emotionally, and intellectually. The mindset to cling to old, antiquated customs and outdated and disproved knowledge that doesn't serve to help us move to a better future has to be abandoned. We have to realize that we are still infants in the world of understanding and that even what we think we know still needs to be examined because it is also in a state of constant change.

We are now at the threshold of our knowledge of the power of the mind; thought; and, especially, our latent psychic powers, including the law of attraction. We are and can become anything our minds can conceive.

Keep an open mind. You will learn something new every day. We each possess the power within our minds and with our thoughts to create a better world, for ourselves as well as for all of humanity.

Your Thoughts Are Gold

The longer I live and think back on all the circumstances I have found myself in and the experiences I have had in my life, the more I see how powerful our mind and thoughts can be. It's a force comparable to electricity. It can't be seen, but its ability to create tangible energy and give force to an endless amount of creations can't be denied. Mind is the source of all power!

Every inanimate object you see around you is alive with the energy and spirit of thought. Every moment I have lived through—joyful, happy, successful times as well as the painful, sad, failures—has been brought about by where my thoughts were and what my mind was envisioning at the time. We all try to find reasons for our circumstances. We give ourselves credit for the good ones and blame the bad ones on something or someone else. The truth is that you have purchased everything in your life. You can have anything you think of, desire, or want to achieve. There are no limits. But you have to be willing to pay the price. The more precious the things you seek, the higher the price. The currency you need and choose to use, be it worthless stones or gold, is abundantly in your possession. You carry gold in the form of commitment, dedication, passion, creativity, and spirit and hard work. You also carry worthless stones in the form of fear, excuses, lazy attitude, doubt, insincerity, and lies.

What do you want and what are you willing to pay for it?

Who Are You Following?

It has been proven that it's easier to con someone than to convince them of the truth. Society has always been prone to follow a leader. The problem has been in its propensity to be easily brainwashed and convinced by colorful lies, exaggeration, and outlandish stories. We all seem to have a need for direction, which leads us to the willingness to fall in line without proper evaluation or investigation of its credibility or solid and verifiable substance.

Nothing helps build a solid character and individual more than taking responsibility for one's own life, successes, and failures. As well-meaning, comforting, and compassionate as someone giving you direction, advice, guidance, assistance, or "helping hand" may seem, a welfare system creates slaves. The minute you are dependent on something or someone's leadership or handouts and people who have no concern or emotional ties to you, you have been enslaved.

Parents are supposed to be a weaning process to this dependency; this is the way of nature. Unfortunately, our traits to be nurtured and cared for can lead us to a detrimental situation of no escape. Every highly successful individual has had to struggle and take the reins in his or her own life. Don't let your life and destiny be controlled or led by someone else's idea of what you should think, do, or want you to be. Break free. It's OK to listen to the advice of others but always make your own final decisions, follow your own path and take responsibility for your own life.

Your Reward

One of the main laws of physics is that to every action there is an equal and opposite reaction. Your success or reward (or what you get from or out of any experience) is equal to what you put into the experience. Your life is the product of the combination of your mind, your speech, and your actions. What you can imagine combined with what you say and the actions you take will create your circumstances.

Our Interdependence

No matter how "self" confident, "self" assured, "self" reliant, "self" motivated, intelligent, talented, creative, or genius you may be, two heads are better than one. Every champion needs a coach.

In every situation, the ability to bounce your ideas of another person; hear another opinion; see another perspective; weigh out different options; or have a round table, think-tank, or review of ideas with one or more people is an asset we can't do without. Every aspect of your life, even when performing or creating something on your own, is an act of interrelation and interaction with others!

In any organization, even the lowest of employees is important. If you didn't have a maintenance man to clean the toilet, the CEO would not be able to think straight if he came out of the bathroom with soiled shoes. In a boxing match, as important as the fighter and his coach are, at a given moment, the guy that brings the water or other equipment to the corner can be crucial. The hand has five fingers, all of them are important; they form a group that provides an ability greater than any individual digit can hope to achieve on its own.

Don't let your ego or pride keep you from appreciating this fact and what every interaction or partnership you have or will ever create in life can and has helped you achieve.

Plan or No Plan

As important as it may be to have viable and solid plans for yourself, for what you will do tomorrow, next week, next month, or next year—or to visualize yourself accomplishing your dreams and where you will be in the future—the only real way to enjoy life is to live in the moment.

Although you may not always win, it's good to have a game plan—your odds of success greatly improve if you know what you need to start. Enthusiasm and passion have to be at the top of your list, but there must also be pliability and spontaneity to your plan.

Zen teaches us that we should experience the now. To really enjoy life you must be in the now—what you are doing this very moment, the now you are sharing with the people around you. Use the situation, circumstances, and opportunities that you have in front of you at this very minute. The Now is all that you really have!

It is said that "the past is gone forever, and the future is not guaranteed." They are both inevitably a creation and consequence of what you are doing now. Flow spontaneously with the moment, each second in order to reach your goal.

Who Are You?

There isn't one of us that has not at some time pondered about who, what, and where we are in our lives. Some of us do it more often than we like to admit.

Every one of us has a specific and personal question, maybe more than just one. Have I made the right decisions with my career? Where will I be next year? Will I achieve the goals I have set for myself? Is my life on the right course? We're all in search of an answer. If we could find a guru, a yogi, a connection to a universal intelligence that could give us the answer or even instructions to a successful life, career, or relationship, our lives would be so easy.

We've all heard the adage "life doesn't come with instructions." So where can we find the answer? The perfect answer is really closer than you think! It is in your own heart and mind. You hold the key that opens up the door to your inspired, creative and empowered self. Your thoughts, words, spirit, and actions are how you engage life.

Not as life is, but as whom you are, renew you! Resolve to Evolve. Enrich your personal life from both a sense of achievement and celebration. You will discover the answer within yourself and create a lifestyle that cultivates fulfillment at every level.

Share a Smile

What could seem like a simple smile to you could bring someone out of a depressing and sad situation. What may seem to you like a simple compliment could make someone feel important or special? What may seem to you like an insignificant conversation or word could mean the world to someone that at that moment needed to hear what you might have to say. We are all different; we share different circumstances in life. We may all look different but we all share one common denominator and that is our emotions. Your emotions create energy and vibrations that can turn a simple encounter into a real connection or relationship. Emotions are the substance of what other people share with us and we share with them. This is the greatest currency that we could ever possess.

Connect with someone today. Either give or receive the most valuable asset you could exchange. The minute you show someone you care about them or need someone to care about you, you open the door to riches beyond your greatest expectations. Enrich someone's life or yours by making that powerful connection.

Bert Rodriguez

Enjoy the Task

You possess the ability to make any task or job you have to do pleasant and rewarding. The poison of dissatisfaction when performing any activity not only affects the final quality of your endeavor, it can keep you from even wanting to complete your goal. By focusing on your final benefit or the original motivation for what you saw yourself accomplishing, you keep a happy attitude while you're in the middle of your struggle. A positive attitude can give you the added energy you need to get you through. The lyrics, "whistle while you work," have true value in keeping you smiling and happy through every day of your life.

You Are Special

We all have a different qualities, talents, and gifts which we can use in life. We are all in different situations and circumstances, but we all possess the same potential and capabilities to improve and rise to higher levels. Don't compare yourself to others. Carefully seek out and discover what you have at your disposal that makes you stand out—makes you different or special—that you can use to help you to achieve your personal goals and your true purpose. Sink all of your commitment into that.

We must take responsibility for doing the best we can with whatever talents we can nurture or develop with what we have each individually been given in our lives.

Be Extraordinary

Don't settle for being "normal." Don't let yourself become complacent and comfortable with the commonplace or ordinary routine in your life. Strive to be Extraordinary. Take the chance and the steps you need to be special; to be everything you know deep inside that you can be; to be the "you" that you were meant to be.

Aspire and do what it takes to be part of the Universal Essence and the Force that gives power and energy to all things in nature, including you. The Force you need to be the extraordinary version of you.

Good or Bad Habits

Any habit, no matter how small, that weakens the will invites other worse habits. Any habit that strengthens the will creates an overall stronger you.

As you perform actions, you create your habits. As you perform your habits, you create your character. As your character performs, you create your destiny. Ever heard the expression "we are creatures of habit"?

Almost 90% of our daily behavior has been developed from the repetition of actions that became habit. The instinct to survive creates habits in every living species. These habits can be beneficial as well as detrimental to our success. People in all fields achieve their goals through consistent, repetitious behavior and through the elimination of bad habits and practice of good habits.

Sacrifice

Sacrifice! How much of your time, of yourself, are you willing to give, to invest, to sacrifice towards something that you want, need, or desire and to your mental, physical, or spiritual improvement? What would you give to have a successful relationship with your health, fitness, career, family, or that special person in your life?

Time is your most valuable asset. It is the one thing you possess that enables you to acquire all your dreams, aspirations, and goals. It is the one thing you can't buy or get back once you've spent it or let it escape your grasp. None of us can know how much of it we have. Cherish it, enjoy every minute of it. Invest it and use it wisely, with focused and loving care. It is the substance and fabric that your happiness, contentment, and memories of who you are, what you have, what you will be, and what you have done with this gift of life are made of.

Think Big

You have to think big, not just about your goals or plans, but about yourself. Who are you? What can you achieve? See yourself bigger than life. See yourself as part of the infinite and universal strength and power that is connected to all of the forces of nature.

Positive and powerful thoughts translate into emotions that release endorphins into your physical being. These, in turn, can give you the drive, energy, and strength that can multiply your abilities and potential. Internalize these thoughts. Visualize yourself hundreds of feet up in the air rising above all your circumstances, problems, and worries. This new perspective will help you see your problems and worries as if they were small details that you can easily maneuver and control. You will then be able to see any obstacle and challenges you may encounter within the scope and reality of your total life as minor insignificant details.

Bert Rodriguez

Don't Get Too Comfortable

We all enjoy a life of leisure and comfort—this is what we work and strive for. But don't let yourself become too comfortable or complacent. Comfort is the enemy of achievement.

Enjoy and appreciate where you are and what you may have accomplished, but don't ever accept it as your limitation. See where you are, not as your limit, but as just another level on your journey before you proceed to the next challenge to reach your highest potential.

Mind Snack

You need to consistently nourish the body as well as the mind. Consume this mental "snack" daily to help strengthen your resolve. "I am on the road to success. No thoughts or circumstances will deter me from reaching my goal."

Bert Rodriguez

Taking Risk

Sometimes taking on a new challenge, changing your routine, or doing something that could improve you may seem uncomfortable—or like you're taking a risk—but that's just a feeling, not a fact. It's just like the feeling of not wanting to step out of your comfort zone that will keep you from going to a higher level; just like the feeling of safety you feel by not trying or embarrassing yourself; just like the depression you will feel by not believing in yourself.

Having the courage to take a risk is just another type of feeling. Everything in life will feel like a risk only because it's unfamiliar. The feeling of taking a risk is the only way for you to reach your highest potential. Feel the greatest thrill you could ever experience. Take the risk.

Exercise Your Brain

If you've ever broken an arm (or another appendage), you probably know what happens to it after four weeks in a cast: It looks atrophied and shrunken and doesn't work well until you start using it again! Any muscle tissue that does not receive stimulation and blood flow deteriorates and dies! This includes your brain! You need to stimulate it to keep it working to the best of its ability.

Learn, read, or practice a new mental function every day. If you don't use it, you lose it!

Bert Rodriguez

Adapting

You have an ingrained human characteristic of adaptability—
you are capable of adapting, whatever the situation. This gives
you tremendous power. To tap into this, you must trust and
believe it! Don't hesitate on starting your project or plans.
Your fears, doubts, and lack of faith squash your potential and
keep you from being your best now and in the future!

Being Spiritual

Religion has gotten a bad rap because of those who abuse it or use it for selfish or self-serving purposes. Everyone chooses an individual way to observe beliefs, having faith in something greater than themselves or in the way they explain or describe an energy or force no one totally comprehends.

Whether you choose to call it God, Universal or Divine Intelligence, Mother Nature, or any other term, don't be judgmental about how others practice the same thing you do. Every great achievement in sports music, art, finances, or any other field was made by an individual that took his thoughts and physical capabilities and was "inspired" (to be in spirit)—or believed or had faith in something greater than himself in order to drive him to achieve it.

Athletes in any sport are inspired and pushed to succeed by their peers, the cheer of the crowd, their fears, their ego or some other emotional motivation. Musicians, artists, and all those who achieve success are also inspired by what they have passion for or what drives them. Respect the way others connect with their spiritual side as much as you do your own!

Bert Rodriguez

Birds of a Feather

If you want to succeed and grow in whatever you do in your life, you need to associate with people who are better than you are at whatever you want to accomplish. You also need to pay attention to those who know more. Observe and take advantage of learning from others that have experienced or possess knowledge you lack. You learn from and become like the people you associate with. Whoever we spend our time with influences us whether we like it or not.

Your Weakest Link

Like the old saying goes, "a chain is only as strong as its weakest link." In order to be truly successful, all aspects of your life should hold to the standards of your utmost behavior and character.

We constantly hear on the news about athletes, stars, politics figures (and other highly accomplished people), who have lost everything because of a weakness in some part of their lives.

We can probably agree that none of us will ever be "perfect" and that not all aspects of our lives will ever be trouble-free. On the other hand, our character and the way we conduct ourselves is the foundation of our success. Character inevitably spills over into all areas of our lives. It is the substance that holds all your links together and gives you your overall and true strength.

Bert Rodriguez

The Perfect Fertilizer

Life will constantly throw dung in your path. You can avoid it along with the people and situations that bring it. You can step in it and carry the stink everywhere you go. Or you can blend with it and use it as fertilizer to grow.

Share Some En-courage-ment

There are three flaws that can be considered at the top of anyone's list in judging an individual's character: The first is being a liar, the second is being a thief, and the third (which can perhaps have the worst stigma) is being a coward.

Conversely, the one thing that can excite and motivate the human spirit to a high point is courage. Courage is a necessary and integral part of success in any endeavor. We all seek and need en-courage-ment. Parents, coaches, teachers, friends, people, or ideals that help us face our challenges with boldness are greatly treasured.

Courage is a virtue we need on a daily basis. By encouraging others you will in turn encourage yourself.

Your Energy Creates

Realize that you are energy. It flows within you like electricity, and you are the light bulb that will illuminate the path you will take. This energy (or electricity) is generated by motivation, inspiration, and encouragement you receive from your thoughts and those of others. Always create and use its power positively.

Your energy creates what you see in the physical world, not the other way around. In other words, energy is the cause; the physical world is the effect. The things that happen in our physical world don't cause our energy; our energy powers the physical things we experience.

Purpose

We should do our best to make every day have purpose—it will give us a sense of accomplishment when we complete our task. Often we get lost in the rat race of the same routine of our goals with work, family, success, and some time to relax and do what we enjoy. Although we try to avoid or ignore it, we can't help but also wonder and seek an answer to the spirit inside us that gives us life and a greater purpose. What is our purpose in this life? This can't be all there is. We're born, we breathe, we live, we love, we suffer, and we die. As we grow older, we can't help but ask ourselves: What is our purpose in this journey called life?

When this question starts a spark in you to discover the answer to what is your individual purpose, it consumes you; it devours you and you become one with it. This very moment is the greatest opportunity you will have to experience the ups and downs that make life interesting, exciting, and worthwhile. Finally discovering the answer and pursuing it with all you've got is where you will find real contentment. Do you know your true purpose?

Have Faith in Yourself

It is tremendously empowering to have faith. It is an immeasurable force that surrounds us and can help us conquer the seemingly impossible. Faith is an invisible power, liken to love, that can give us the inspiration and strength to "move mountains." It is therefore extremely important to have faith in ourselves and our purpose.

Your faith and what you truly believe may very well give you the ability to "move mountains," but you are expected to bring tools.

Tap into the Force

We are part of and are connected to a universal intelligence. It can help guide us and give us what we need to get through the challenges we may face in life. When someone says, "God, please help me," the Force hears you and will respond. It might also let you practically drown because you are on this earth to learn; to survive; to sink or swim; to build your own boat and row it. Your best efforts must combine themselves with this force in order to reach your goals.

Bert Rodriguez

Be a Seed

The biggest oak was once a sprout—a tiny seed. You carry a seed in you. A seed of commitment, passion, drive, self-respect, love, caring, compassion, and goodness in that is in you. Plant this seed, Nurture it, water it, feed it daily, let your positive attitude shine on it like the bright light of the sun and watch it grow.

Etch A Sketch

Just like an Etch A Sketch, your thoughts create a vibrating frequency that pinpoints and magnetically pulls together the particles of energy needed to manifest into reality what your mind sees. Your thoughts will fill in the details of the picture you want. The more you focus on this vibrating frequency to trace the exact vision that you hold in your mind, the more specifically your life will attract, reflect, and solidify to the picture you envision and the things you desire, want to be, or want to experience.

Bert Rodriguez

Follow Your Dreams

The bulk of your friends and family—be it because of their own fears and concerns that you don't experience the pain of failure or because their ego would be destroyed to see you rise above what they have barely managed to accomplish—are "Dream Killers." If choosing your dreams over the company of these people means your life will be void of their particular close friendships or relations, without hesitation choose following your dreams. But if you can find one person that believes in you, always supports and encourages you in spite of your failures or apparent lack of qualifications, cherish them dearly and keep that person near. They are a diamond in the mountain of dull black coal you may have to climb. Their brilliant reflection will be all you need to light the path on the journey to achieving your dreams.

Repair Yourself with Gold

Karatsu is the Japanese art of repairing broken vases with gold. Don't let the fact that you may have fallen—been cracked or broken—keep you from acquiring an even greater quality. Bond yourself back up with the gold found in positive thoughts and affirmations deep within you that will give you a greater sense of worth than you ever had. Let yourself and those that may have not seen your strength, resilience, and the true potential appreciate and see that you can come back with more value and beauty than you or anyone ever thought possible.

You Are a Warrior

We are all given and are in possession of a bow and arrow with which to survive the adventure that is our life's quest. We must maintain our focused attention, use the strength of our expectations to draw on the bow of our ability to totally control our thoughts and accurately shoot the arrow of our intent. This is required of us as true warriors and necessary in order for us to successfully hit the targets bulls eye that are our goals.

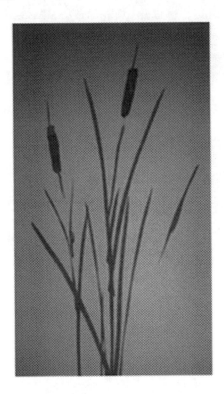

Kicking Butt (But)

I often describe my journey in Martial Arts as one of first thinking that it was about kicking someone else's butt then realizing that it was about kicking my own butt and more importantly kicking life's butt. I finally reached the enlightened thought that it's actually aout kicking life's "But's"

The ones that come up every time we want to achieve or do something like starting a new business, reaching a goal, taking on a new challenge yet don't because we always end our thoughts or statement with a "Yeah but" and the add the excuse that we use as the reason why we think we can't or shouldn't.

Eliminate the word –But- from your vocabulary and you will amaze yourself at how much farther ahead you will get and how much more you will accomplish.

Bert Rodriguez

Wisdom

Knowledge in a given subject is something that is available and can be acquired by anyone willing to dedicate the time and effort. Wisdom—the ability to use what is learned to benefit an individual or society—generally speaking, is not.

Throughout history, the necessary data and facts needed for every great invention and advancement was there for all to use, but the wisdom to put it together, to create, was possessed by a rare few. The ability to be creative, inspired, or tap into a greater universal intelligence, force, and power will elude all but those that can see and appreciate the spiritual or inspirational side of life and all creation. Learned, memorized, or acquired knowledge may only result in limited intelligence or talent. The ability to take and pass a test, earn a degree, or work as a doctor, a lawyer, a teacher, professor, or any other profession, does not equate to competence. Insight, good judgment, and wisdom are things few ever achieve.

Law of Attraction

Our lives can be enhanced as we engage universal laws that have attracting Power. Through the practice of these principles, we unleash the magnetic ability that has always been at our disposal. It is no accident that we fail or succeed. Our success or failure centers on the right application of natural laws, principles, and the strategies behind our hearts desire. We will attract what is in our thoughts and what is emotionally connected to our subconscious mind. Positive, constructive, and assuring thoughts will manifest themselves in your life as surely as self-defeating ones will. You can accomplish everything your mind conceives through the strength of the universal force that is in you, in all of nature and is part of all things we experience.

Your Shortcomings

Accept and be comfortable with what you may perceive as a shortcoming in life. The Tao teaches us that the more you have, the more you need to protect and the more you have to lose. The higher you are, the further down you can fall. The tallest tree is the first one to get cut down. The crooked, bent tree is of no use to the woodsman so it lives a thousand years. To become straight, appreciate being bent. To become full, be empty. Be like water, but don't always worry about having to make big waves. Sometimes just flow down to fill the emptiness of the smallest place. Appreciate the now, where and who you are. This is the secret to contentment and success.

Pessimist or Optimist

Pessimism and the need to have the answer to our problems clearly laid out and proven before they can be accepted stems from self-doubt and fear. To believe and optimistically approach what is not certain evolves from the ability to discern, self-confidence and faith in ourselves and in what for the moment may not seem clear.

Bert Rodriguez

Your Rope

Life is like a rope, sometimes it gives you slack, sometimes it pulls tight. Both times you can use it to either pull you forward or up to greater heights or to tie yourself in knots and keep you from moving.

The Warrior Within

To be a true warrior, to conquer, to be able to win, to destroy the enemy or any situation it is necessary to be willing to sacrifice yourself to the death for what you commit to. Your word to yourself and to others and your honor should be worth more than life itself. You must be willing to live and die by this code. It will be the foundation of everything that you do. Don't talk a game you are not willing to back up. Accept and welcome the moment and whatever you may confront. Living by this code will give you the ability to appreciate every day you are on this earth and everything you accomplish.

We want to feel like winners, not losers. Sometimes we fail to realize how this internal power trumps any physical or tangible strength. It gives us dominance over ourselves and the ability to face what may seem like failure or potential defeat and rise to the highest level. This is what gave the Samurai, Japanese Kamikazes, and any individual who has risked mental, emotional or physical death to achieve great success their true power.

Bert Rodriguez

Becoming the Best You

When you participate, train, or compete in any physical or mental activity, sports, or challenge, don't necessarily do it to be an Einstein, a rocket scientist, an Arnold Schwarzenegger, James Bond, Bruce Lee, Adonis look-alike, or to be a world champion. You should do it to learn the value of commitment and dedication, courage, discipline, determination, achievement, being able to take physical and emotional pain, losing, or failure and still not giving up. Do it to help you conquer the fear and overcome the real challenges you face in life. Stay on course but realize and appreciate the true meaning and value in the total of all your efforts.

Worry and Regret

It is pointless and a waste of mental and physical energy to worry about things that might or might not materialize in the future. It may actually bring forth the very thing we fear and would want to avoid by the law of attraction. Our mind creates a magnetic energy by what we consistently hold in our thoughts. Regret is also useless and destructive in that we cannot change what has already occurred in the past. Regret will drain us of the life force and thoughts we could use to bring forth benefits in the future.

Keep your thoughts positive, constructive and in the moment. Your mind and body's energy needs to be used and will serve you better for what is happening in the now.

Making Adjustments

We often need to make adjustments on the way to our goals, but few of us are willing to make radical changes in our lives.

How your life unfolds when you let chance determine your choices or say "let's see what happens" is fate. Your true and fulfilled destiny will reveal itself to you when you confront your fears and make a conscious decision to "make things happen."

Be willing to make adjustments. The ability to make the best of a bad situation will empower your future.

The Warrior That Is You

We are all warriors—and the heroes or cowards—of our individual lives. We may all evolve differently but are the same in that we all must confront our own personal dragons and demons. Our obstacles take the form of problems and stress that help us gain a higher degree of mental, physical, and spiritual power. We can benefit from or misuse and waste these challenges and experiences.

A warrior's true purpose in life is to grow in wisdom, understanding, and consciousness—to grow and take on his or her responsibilities, have respect and love towards themselves as well as towards others, and ultimately share and pass on the gauntlet of what they have conquered and learned. These are the true badges of courage.

Visualization

You should believe in and practice the power that thought and visualization have in creating new circumstances, your physical abilities, or the tangible things in your life. There has been extensive research that supports the idea of how the linking of visualization tremendously improves motivation, confidence and performance, and the quality of the final product.

The Right Time

When the things you are working hard to achieve, desire, or expecting or waiting for don't seem to be happening, it can be a sign that the right time and conditions for something greater have not yet arrived. The more that you seize and take advantage of the opportunity, continue to believe in what you can do, and remain focused, the more those positive thoughts will draw you closer to your goals.

Impatience, doubt, and ungratefulness (regarding your experiences) are negative thoughts that will attract more negative things to your life. Appreciating what you are going through, no matter how hard it may seem, could be the lesson you need learn. Enduring this scenario may give you the strength you will need to acquire the things that you want.

By finding the value and enjoying even the simplest things and being in the moment you will give off the vibrations that will in turn create the positive circumstances that will lead you to those bigger and greater things that you seek.

Bert Rodriguez

Be Fearless

To achieve real success in any endeavor you choose, you must be fearless and have courage. What others may perceive as impulsive or even reckless may be essential. Playing it safe can sometimes slow you down and keep you from taking advantage of opportunities or just keep you from ever taking that first step.

Bravely face your challenge. Believe in yourself. Have the confidence to trust your ability to conquer any obstacle you may encounter. Use this formula to go beyond your natural capabilities, talents, and potential. Be fearless. The main obstacle to overcoming any of the problems you may face is not having the courage to challenge them.

Work the Force

You must subconsciously and with all your heart sincerely believe and trust that the same force and power that moves the world can also work on your behalf. Confidence and faith in this powerful thought can and will increase your ability to objectify all that you envision and desire.

Bert Rodriguez

What Do You Deserve?

We have probably all at one time or another used the expression "I didn't deserve that" or "I deserve better." Karma and the balance of how life gives you back what you put into it are not dealt back on singular instances or case by case basis but instead on the whole of all your actions.

If we all got back what we truly deserved for the total of all our positive efforts—or what we may have done diligently, with commitment, and effectively—balanced against the negative of what we have neglected, done haphazardly, done poorly, or totally ignored, we would probably all be in the negative. Because of the law of diminishing return, we need to put forward more effort and do more than we will ever get back or expect. Always put forward 150%.

Appreciate and be thankful for whatever you are able to reap from what you have sown. Never stop trying to outdo or improve on what you can produce, create, or put into everything you do in life.

Sunshiny Day

If you start the morning out with a negative attitude, there is no hope for a positive day. Expect and look for the sun to shine down and brighten your every moment.

Bert Rodriguez

The Rhythm of Life

We associate rhythm with the flow of music, the beating of drums, and the movement of the body in dance, but everything in life has its own rhythm.

Rhythm can be found in the way a business makes profits and then loses a fortune; within growing and prospering of a home, a town, or city and then the deterioration or abandonment of those places. There is a rhythm in friendships, love, and health of flourishing and declining. There is the rhythm of life and death. There is a rhythm of your emotions. There is a rhythm in your life of good things happening, then flowing to bad, to nothing happening at all. There is a rhythm of loud noise to soft sounds to total silence to quiet and peace. And then the rhythms are repeated.

To enjoy music, you must appreciate its rhythm, including the space where no rhythm is heard. Listen carefully and tune into the rhythm of life. Without this rhythm, there is nothing but dead silence. This is the rhythm of life.

Imagine the Ridiculous

It baffles the mind to stop and think of all the things someone's imagination has produced—from the ridiculous to the sublime. We are surrounded by and enjoy a myriad of things that were imagined in thought and seemed, from a logical point of view, to be impossible, far-fetched, crazy, or ridiculous. Don't limit your goals, dreams, and potential with what you see only with your normal vision. Let your eyes observe your life through glasses that can see past the limited perspective of what is commonplace or obvious. Magnify what you see by using the lens of an insanely wild imagination. Have the audacity to imagine the unimaginable. Let loose the child that you were the first time you finger painted the most wonderful creation that you could ever think of and recall how proud you and everyone who saw it was. Have fun as you create the masterpiece that can be your life.

Cultivating Your Life

Your thoughts, your emotions, and your soul will attract what you love as well as what you fear. These are your two most dominant emotions. Your outer circumstances are shaped and greatly influenced by what you cultivate within. These will run the spectrum from joyful and blissful to painful and unpleasant. Cultivate love, not fear. Let these give you the roots that will give your aspirations and life the strong foundation it needs for your continued growth.

The Ego

Perhaps the biggest obstacle for our ability to make significant progress in any area of our lives is our emotion of ego. Our pride and the desire to not feel or look incompetent or failing to ourselves or others keeps us from taking the necessary risk and make the mistakes that are may be necessary for us to align ourselves with success. Nothing can be achieved or perfected to a high degree without some failure along the way.

Bert Rodriguez

Anger

When having to deal with problems or negative situations that appear in our lives, anger is usually viewed as a negative. Actually it can be a positive place to experience. It means you are moving forward. Before you feel anger, you find yourself in a place of helplessness. It is part of a cycle or path you have to take in order to reach completeness with whatever is affecting the moment, get through it, and put it behind you. It is like crossing a dangerous creek to reach the other side and be on solid ground again.

View the anger as one of the stones you need to step on and use to get past the obstacle that is in your path. It is not somewhere where you want to stand, remain, or become part of. It's just something you need to step on to move forward. See it and turn it into something useful that you need to get back on solid ground.

By not being caught in and overwhelmed by its negative side, you will create a situation where you use it to benefit you and move forward.

The Fear of Choices

Wherever in life you find yourself, you got there by making choices—not one big choice but tens of hundreds of small choices. Similar to the way that individual molecules one by one make up the structure and integrity of an object, your simple, sometimes moment-to-moment choices make up who are, who you can be, and who you will be in the future.

The emotions associated with making these decisions have a tremendous influence on the things you choose, the ones you didn't choose, and on their outcomes. You possess unbelievable potential, talents, and possibilities, but you must first face your fears about making these choices.

Bert Rodriguez

Life's Harmony

Our wishes, desires, circumstances, and goals will come to fruition only when they are in harmony with our thoughts and actions and our character. We all anxiously try to improve our situations but totally ignore the importance of first working on taking ourselves to a higher level.

The Genius in You

Genius is a state of consciousness. Those that tap in to it give credit to a higher influence or Universal Intelligence. They become detached from ego and possess an air of humility by realizing that their gifts come from an outside force.

Those who distinguish themselves with true genius in music, mathematics, science, in any field or in daily life, describe their talent, work or inspiration coming to them in a vision, dream or sudden revelation. Genius is like an inner unseen invisible force that inspires tangible creations or manifestations. It is a relation with a higher vibration or frequency.

The law of Yin and Yang dictates that we are all different yet all the same, both physically and mentally. We can each develop in our own way and at different levels the ability to attract and tune into the genius that is part of the universal Essence and connects us all as human beings.

Bert Rodriguez

Success

True success is working at something that you love and have passion for. If it is something that benefits and helps others, you will find fortune and riches not only in tangible form but in a value that cannot be measured in silver and gold.

Will Power

You can be strong, you can be weak.

You can advance, you can retreat.

You can feel love, you can feel hate.

You can agree, you can debate.

You can move forward, you can be still.

It all depends upon your will.

Go Power

Your thoughts, your efforts to turn them into reality and the emotional content you fuel them with will create your experiences of success or of failure in your life.

Recharge Yourself

In these hectic and busy times we are constantly surrounded by people and busy with situations that are sometimes beyond our control. We all need a little push, a pat on the back, or just a little encouragement. But even when someone tries their best to cheer you on or say something they feel will help you move forward, it seems it's of little help.

This is the moment that can be of benefit to you if you realize that for all intents and purposes, you are basically alone in this big world.

It can be just the time you need to connect with yourself and go to that special place that encourages, motivates, empowers, and gives you the boost you need to carry on. No one else has a greater connection to the universal essence, force and power that is all around us than you. You need this solitude and alone time to be able to tap into it mentally, emotionally, and spiritually

Bert Rodriguez

This Life

Do not leave this earth without first living out the adventure that you envisioned your life to be. Never live in fear of failure or doubt of the challenges you may face or of what you know you are capable of being. Use every day to the fullest. Never let yourself cower to whatever obstacles may stand in your way.

Find a way to conquer and complete every goal your mind has ever dreamed of. Don't let yourself burnout your remaining years slowly like a candle but fly to your greatest heights like an invincible dragon, burst into flames and come down in a fiery blaze of glory and let yourself reappear like the legendary phoenix.

Your #1 Goal

In competition of any kind, as well as in life, you have numerous goals you will want or need to attain. To come out ahead, to succeed, to follow your game plan, to use one technique or another, to achieve a personal best, to avoid injury, the list can be diverse and endless. As important as all these points may be, trying to focus on too many goals can keep you from accomplishing any of them.

The one key to conquering any and all activities you take on is to keep an inner calm and composed mind. This should be your number one goal and the one thing that will bring forth all the physical strengths, training, and preparations you have been working on. Don't let a cluttered or scattered mind stop you in your tracks

Bert Rodriguez

Disagreements

In order for us to come to mutual terms, find peace, settle an argument, make up with a friend, family member, loved one, or even a perceived enemy, we must see, appreciate, and accept the countless ways we relate, how we are alike, how we need, and can be beneficial to each other and our harmonious existence.

Learning

The best teachers teach not by sharing what they know with others but by practicing what they know with themselves and living as examples. The best students learn not by absorbing or memorizing information but by using what they learn in their lives and sharing it with others.

We are in the same stroke both teachers and students. What we learn from others we have to teach to ourselves and what we teach ourselves we have to learn from others. We teach what we need to learn and learn what we need to teach.

Bert Rodriguez

Go For It

As you recall the final outcome of the chances you had to go higher in life or reach a particular goal, you will not be disappointed with the things that didn't work out, the bruises, blisters or failures you had to endure. But you will most certainly regret the things you didn't at least make the effort to go for. The ones you wanted, felt you could have accomplished but were too afraid to try."

Life Coach

Every champion needs a coach. We hire and use coaches in education, finances, sports, music, art and every other area where we need to develop and improve. Remember that the most important thing you are working on to take to a higher level is your life. Seek out someone you respect and trust that can help you focus and bring out your talents and ability to achieve your goal.

Bert Rodriguez

How You Perform

The effort you put into any task you take on, regardless of its size or importance, how simple or how complicated, is a visual portrait and a written statement of your character and the kind of individual you are.

Forgiveness

Everyone of us have had someone in our lives that has hurt, abused, let us down or taken advantage of our love or kindness.

It's impossible for us to wish for or exchange the past for a better yesterday. All we have is tomorrow. In order for us to find happiness we have to find forgiveness in our own heart not just for them, but also for ourselves, and for the pain and bitterness we carry inside us in order to move forward

Bert Rodriguez

Your Fight

After training so many athletes for their particular challenge, goal or world title I use the analogy when counseling or working with others in different areas that we are all in constant preparation for our own struggle or world class fight. Our fight to succeed, to better ourselves, sometimes it's a fight to just get out of bed in the morning. We are in a fight to conquer and win over daily problems with our finances, relationships, as parents, students, life partners, or just to be happy.

We are inside the ring called life. By ourselves, alone, no one but us and the opposition. We have to remember our training. Our commitment, our goal, our purpose, the big prize. We must draw on our courage, our passion, our do or die attitude to succeed. We cannot let fear, doubt pain or struggle overtake our biggest strength, the will to win.! That what I tell them, what I tell myself, what the voice in your corner, your trainer, your biggest ally and fan, your own mind, needs to tell you. And you must listen! Be the champion you know you can be. You can do it Rocky.

Slip Sliding Away

Simon and Garfunkel had a hit song back in the 70s called Slip Sliding Away. The lyrics said, 'You know the nearer your destination the more you slip sliding away'. I love this song it speaks the greatest of truths. This is the story of our lives. By the time we learn the lessons we need and are fulfilling our dreams and goals, our lives are well on their way and the time we have to enjoy our achievements is almost over. Cherish and celebrate and enjoy every day, every moment, every failure, every success and everyone that shared them with you as well. They are the most wonderful part of the journey you are on

A Healthier Happier You

To benefit from and enjoy a vibrant, high energy lifestyle your motives, commitment and sense of purpose must be in total alignment. Your thoughts as well as your attitude will stimulate your brain to release endorphins that will give you the boost and strength needed to achieve your goal. But it must be driven by a total and sincere desire to change, improve and take yourself to your highest level of physical and mental condition and existence. Hold dear and treat with care your greatest possession in life.

Ups and Downs

Nature's law of negative and positive cannot be denied or controlled. There can't be a sunrise without a sunset. There can't be a beginning without an end. There can't be life without death. There is as much pain and suffering in birth and living as there is peace and joy in old age and dying. Yet we fear and desperately fight aging and the deterioration of our bodies and try to put off, ignore and not accept the inevitable fact that death will consume us all. We want to live forever. Not being at one with this flow and balance in all things is like trying to smooth out agitated water with your hands.

Creating Castles

At times, it will seem like it's taking forever for things to happen or for you to complete your project. But it's not forever. Your life, in relation to time, is over in the blink of an eye. Each minute, each hour, each day that goes by is a precious gift. These days are the building blocks you will use to construct the castles that are your dreams and aspirations.

The consistency with which we use each of our days to create what we strive for and desire is important. They are scarce! The longer you put off your goals, the less chance you have of ever achieving them. Every day you let slip by, like misplaced bricks without mortar, will turn to dust.

I have had the opportunity to participate in and attend marathons where thousands of people start, and before the first mile, hundreds find some excuse not to continue. How many people apply to colleges and how many follow through and graduate? How many types of businesses open every day, and how many make it past the first year?

Of course, you can always find an excuse and call it "a good reason." Many of us praise and give ourselves the credit when things go right but blame our misfortunes or failures on someone or something else.

The truth is, somewhere during the process, we didn't use enough building blocks or tossed them haphazardly at dreams to see if we might get a chance hit. Or we hope that our building blocks might fall into the right place. Don't count on it. These blocks which represent commitment, consistency, and effort must be handled with great care. They must be put in the right place so that we never have to regret how or why they were used. Most of us have had the time to lay the foundations for our castles. How strong is yours?

You still have time. Stay on that road. Walk it often. Stick with it. Maintain the commitment to your goals, your work, your friends, your family, your business, and your life.

Believe in and tap into the supernatural powers that we all possess. Discover how you can enjoy the happiness and fulfillment that creating your destiny will bring.

CHAPTER THREE

THE TEN STEPS TO SUCCESS

When you need to achieve a goal—whether it's starting a new business, moving to a new home, baking a cake, or buying a new car—it's sometimes hard to know where to begin. Many of us have a tendency to be overwhelmed. We wonder to ourselves: Where do I begin? What's the best approach? What will do I need to succeed? I developed The Ten Steps to Success as a simple guideline for achieving successful outcomes to any goal.

The Ten Steps to Success

1. Knowledge
2. Answer
3. Experience
4. Balance
5. Mobility
6. Range
7. Stance
8. Timing
9. Speed
10. Strength

We will discuss each of the Ten Steps one at a time as they would relate to four example endeavors. You will notice with different subjects the concerns will be identical. This is one of the effects of yin and yang, where everything is different, but everything is the same. See if you can find other points or details to add to the three subjects being discussed. Also, note how it would seem necessary to follow the sequence from beginning to end. A harmonious interaction between the steps has to occur because to not simultaneously consider all steps would not follow a synchronous flow. Although the saying goes, "You can't put the cart before the horse," before you begin you actually have to review and consider all ten and see how they would differ, compliment, be in harmony with, strengthen and or relate to one another. The final "strength" or quality of whatever the endeavor will be subject to the strength, quality, and consequence of the integral parts covered from one to ten.

To better understand how to apply The Ten Steps to Success in your own life, we will review three examples labeled A, B, and C. Here are the three example endeavors I will explain and illustrate using the Ten Steps:

Example A: Putting together a party or event for yourself or someone else.

Example B: Starting a business.

Example C: Preparing a battle plan to settle a dispute between two countries that border each other.

Before we start to apply our Ten Steps and compare our three examples, we will use the analogy of baseball and swinging the bat with the intent of hitting the pitched ball preferably scoring a home run. This will give us a quick overview of the anomaly found in The Ten Steps.

The two main talents consistently used to distinguish a good athlete are to be strong and fast. You will notice that strength is tenth on the list and speed is ninth in order of their real importance.

Hitting the ball with a lot of force, power, or "Strength," would be considered as the best way to achieve this goal, but regardless of how hard one swings the bat without the speed to match the incoming ball the consequence will be nothing more than a strike.

Once we have the "Speed" to match the speed of the pitch, which is usually the second most attributed characteristic to a good athlete, it also becomes superfluous if the "Timing" of the swing is not considered perfect.

The "Timing, Speed, and Strength" needed are dependent on a proper "Stance" without which makes the later three impossible to achieve. These four cannot be controlled unless the "Range" of the bat is in perfect position or distance with the body as well as with the direction the batter wants to send the ball and in order to put correct body core into the swing.

These five cannot be achieved if the batter does not possess the smooth "Mobility" required of his limbs and body.

All of these, especially smooth mobility are impossible without a harmonious "Balance" between the batter, his mind, body, the bat, the ball, and the pitcher.

The more "Experience" the player has, whether it is from his own practice or the experience of a good coach, the greater his ability to complete steps three through ten will be.

Of course, the quality and usefulness of steps two through nine are solidified in effectiveness by step number one, "Knowledge." Understanding, considering, and applying all Ten Steps diligently will be the best way for the player to achieve the success of hitting a home run and will be the true measure of his strength!

Putting the Ten Steps Into Practice

Now let's use the Ten Steps applied to our three examples.

STEP ONE: Knowledge

A. <u>Putting together a party</u>: You have to have knowledge of the type of party—or what exactly you are celebrating—as well as how to plan and arrange a successful party and all the particulars and specific details (the age and number of planned attendees, etc.).

B. <u>Starting a business</u>: You have to have knowledge about the type of business you wish to start (potential for profits, competition, the need for particular product or services, the capital needed, etc.).

C. <u>Preparing a battle strategy</u>: You have to have knowledge of combatants, their dispute, their tactics, the number of combatants, arsenal, training, mindset, etc.

STEP TWO: Answer

A. <u>Party or celebration</u>: Laying out your plan, entertainment, the age of participants, day or night gathering, likes and dislikes of attendees, etc.

B. <u>Starting a business</u>: How or where to acquire funds, exact startup cost, competition, suppliers, profit-and-loss margin, history of similar businesses, best location, etc.

C. <u>Preparing a battle strategy</u>: Establishing the logistics; understanding the details of the dispute, the mindset of both sides involved, what resolution would be acceptable to both sides, etc.

STEP THREE: Experience

A. <u>Putting together a party</u>: Do you need a party planner, do you have experience or have someone that has been successful at putting one together.

B. <u>Starting a business</u>: Do you have experience in the type of business or someone that will know or have the skills required to organize it or its operation, etc.?

C. <u>Preparing a battle strategy</u>: Do you have experienced soldiers, officers, track record or similar to draw successful operational plans from?

STEP FOUR: Balance

A. <u>Putting together a party</u>: Do you have everything you need: supplies, guest list, location, etc.?

B. <u>Starting a business</u>: Do you have start-up funds, a location, employees, product/merchandise, equipment, etc.?

C. <u>Preparing a battle strategy</u>: Do you have all the needed soldiers, supply rations, weapons, ammunition, gear, etc.?

STEP FIVE: Mobility

A. <u>Putting together a party</u>: Do you have the ability to move your supplies and other necessities like chairs, tables, refreshments, and ice to your location. Will everyone have the ability to get to or reach the location, etc.?

B. <u>Starting a business</u>: Will your type of clients be able to reach and easily get to your place of business. Will your suppliers be able to come in and out or be in proximity to your place? Will the operation process move smoothly and efficiently?

C. <u>Preparing a battle strategy</u>: Are you able to reach and control surrounding area efficiently and effectively? Will you have the necessary transportation for your people, equipment, weapons, supplies, etc.?

STEP SIX: Range

A. <u>Putting together a party</u>: Is it close or in proximity enough to your guest, convenient for everyone to come, i.e. in the neighborhood or reachable by highways, roads, interstate, etc.)?

B. <u>Starting a business</u>: Is it in proximity to the type of clients you need, employees you will use, and in an area where your services would be warranted or needed?

C. <u>Preparing a battle strategy</u>: Where will you set up camp? Will you be in correct proximity to the locations of engagement or close enough to deploy your forces in due time and efficiently to the front lines? Will you be in proximity to be able to re-supply supply your forces if necessary?

STEP SEVEN: Stance

A. <u>Putting together a party</u>: How big of a place will you require? How should you decorate your location and should it be outdoors, indoors, in a big hall, etc.?

B. <u>Starting a business:</u> Should it be a storefront on a main street, an office space, in a large building? Will you need a location that is on a main floor, etc.?

C. <u>Preparing a battle strategy</u>: How and where should you set up camp? Where will you store/set up weapons and supplies? Have you identified perimeters, etc.?

STEP EIGHT: Timing

A. <u>Putting together a party</u>: What month week or time should it be held? How long should it last? How much preparation time do you need? How long of an advance notice to guests, etc.?

B. <u>Starting a business</u>: How long will be needed to prepare and set up location? When should we open—what hours, what days, etc.?

C. <u>Preparing a battle strategy</u>: How much time do we have to plan, prepare, and execute? How long should we pursue objective? What time should we engage the enemy (day or night; what time of the year)? What will the weather conditions, terrain, and other similar conditions be or what do you require, etc.?

STEP NINE: Speed

A. <u>Putting together a party</u>: How much time is needed for preparation? How much lead time do you need to secure location, supplies, guest notifications, food and drink orders, etc.?

B. <u>Starting a business</u>: Do we have a deadline we must quickly consider for construction, permits, utilities, loans, suppliers, etc.?

C. <u>Preparing a battle strategy</u>: At what pace or how quickly do we need to deploy or execute maneuvers? Can we approach slowly with caution and with stealth, etc.?

STEP TEN: Strength

A. <u>Putting together a party</u>: How much money, supplies, chairs, tables, or help will be needed to prepare the location, carry supplies, serve guests, or clean up after, etc.?

B. <u>Starting a business</u>: How much financing, employees, equipment, supplies, etc., will be needed?

C. <u>Preparing a battle strategy</u>: How strong a force is needed to execute the plan; set up equipment; prepare/store ammunition? How much force is necessary (or warranted)? Will a show of strength be sufficient, or will we have to engage in strong attack, etc.?

In every case, the strength to be considered is actually found in measuring the outcome or results perhaps more so than the strength needed to accomplish the task. Try applying the Ten Steps to any project you have and see how it will apply and help you prepare a better plan.

A FINAL NOTE

It is my deepest desire that you find these thoughts useful and beneficial—that by contemplating and applying these quotes you are able to use them to find a beneficial peace. Use whatever wisdom you can extract from them to help you deal with your own mind, emotions, and feelings that are at the root of all the decisions you need to make which mold and shape your life and bring you the contentment that we all seek.

We are what we think. All that we are arises with our thoughts. With our thoughts, we make the world.

-Buddha

ACKNOWLEDGEMENTS

I would like to thank Heather Field for her help in editing this book. Her suggestions, corrections, and ideas helped make the book into something I am proud to share.

For inquiries, questions, comments or copies of this publication contact:

Master Bert Rodriguez
Email: realbxrs@gmail.com
Phone: (954) 232-2248

Printed in the United States
By Bookmasters